Library of
Davidson College

TAX REFORM FOR A PRODUCTIVE ECONOMY

A Statement by the
Research and Policy Committee of the
Committee for Economic Development

October 1985

336.2
C7342t

ISBN: 0-87186-081-3

PRICE: $5.00

86-2485

COMMITTEE FOR ECONOMIC DEVELOPMENT
477 Madison Avenue, New York, N.Y. 10022 / (212) 688-2063
1700 K Street, N.W., Washington, D.C. 20006 / (202) 296-5860

CED COUNTERPART ORGANIZATIONS IN FOREIGN COUNTRIES

Close relations exist between the Committee for Economic Development and independent, nonpolitical research organizations in other countries. Such counterpart groups are composed of business executives and scholars and have objectives similar to those of CED, which they pursue by similarly objective methods. CED cooperates with these organizations on research and study projects of common interest to the various countries concerned. This program has resulted in a number of joint policy statements involving such international matters as energy, East-West trade, assistance to the developing countries, and the reduction of nontariff barriers to trade.

CE	Círculo de Empresarios Serrano Jover 5-2°, Madrid 8, Spain
CEDA	Committee for Economic Development of Australia 139 Macquarie Street, Sydney 2001, New South Wales, Australia
CEPES	Europäische Vereinigung für Wirtschaftliche und Soziale Entwicklung Reuterweg 14, 6000 Frankfurt/Main, West Germany
IDEP	Institut de l'Entreprise 6, rue Clément-Marot, 75008 Paris, France
経済同友会	Keizai Doyukai (Japan Committee for Economic Development) Japan Industrial Club Bldg. 1 Marunouchi, Chiyoda-ku, Tokyo, Japan
PSI	Policy Studies Institute 100, Park Village East, London NW1 3SR, England
SNS	Studieförbundet Näringsliv och Samhälle Sköldungagatan 2, 11427 Stockholm, Sweden

The Management and Financing of Colleges *(1973)*
Strengthening the World Monetary System *(1973)*
Financing the Nation's Housing Needs *(1973)*
Building a National Health-Care System *(1973)*
*A New Trade Policy Toward Communist Countries *(1972)*
High Employment Without Inflation:
  A Positive Program for Economic Stabilization *(1972)*
Reducing Crime and Assuring Justice *(1972)*
Military Manpower and National Security *(1972)*
The United States and the European Community:
  Policies for a Changing World Economy *(1971)*
Improving Federal Program Performance *(1971)*
Social Responsibilities of Business Corporations *(1971)*
Education for the Urban Disadvantaged:
  From Preschool to Employment *(1971)*
Further Weapons Against Inflation *(1970)*
Making Congress More Effective *(1970)*
Training and Jobs for the Urban Poor *(1970)*
Improving the Public Welfare System *(1970)*
Reshaping Government in Metropolitan Areas *(1970)*
Economic Growth in the United States *(1969)*
Assisting Development in Low-Income Countries *(1969)*
*Nontariff Distortions of Trade *(1969)*
Fiscal and Monetary Policies for Steady Economic Growth *(1969)*
Financing a Better Election System *(1968)*
Innovation in Education: New Directions for the American School *(1968)*
Modernizing State Government *(1967)*
*Trade Policy Toward Low-Income Countries *(1967)*
How Low Income Countries Can Advance Their Own Growth *(1966)*
Modernizing Local Government *(1966)*
Budgeting for National Objectives *(1966)*

*Statements issued in association with CED counterpart organizations in foreign countries.

STATEMENTS ON NATIONAL POLICY ISSUED BY THE RESEARCH AND POLICY COMMITTEE

SELECTED PUBLICATIONS

Tax Reform for a Productive Economy *(1985)*

Investing in Our Children: Business and the Public Schools *(1985)*

Fighting Federal Deficits: The Time for Hard Choices *(1984)*

Strategy for U.S. Industrial Competitiveness *(1984)*

Strengthening the Federal Budget Process:
A Requirement for Effective Fiscal Control *(1983)*

Productivity Policy: Key to the Nation's Economic Future *(1983)*

Energy Prices and Public Policy *(1982)*

Public-Private Partnership: An Opportunity for Urban Communities *(1982)*

Reforming Retirement Policies *(1981)*

Transnational Corporations and Developing Countries: New Policies for a Changing World Economy *(1981)*

Fighting Inflation and Rebuilding a Sound Economy *(1980)*

Stimulating Technological Progress *(1980)*

Helping Insure Our Energy Future:
A Program for Developing Synthetic Fuel Plants Now *(1979)*

Redefining Government's Role in the Market System *(1979)*

Improving Management of the Public Work Force:
The Challenge to State and Local Government *(1978)*

Jobs for the Hard-to-Employ:
New Directions for a Public-Private Partnership *(1978)*

An Approach to Federal Urban Policy *(1977)*

Key Elements of a National Energy Strategy *(1977)*

The Economy in 1977–78: Strategy for an Enduring Expansion *(1976)*

Nuclear Energy and National Security *(1976)*

Fighting Inflation and Promoting Growth *(1976)*

Improving Productivity in State and Local Government *(1976)*

*International Economic Consequences of High-Priced Energy *(1975)*

Broadcasting and Cable Television:
Policies for Diversity and Change *(1975)*

Achieving Energy Independence *(1974)*

A New U.S. Farm Policy for Changing World Food Needs *(1974)*

Congressional Decision Making for National Security *(1974)*

*Toward a New International Economic System:
A Joint Japanese-American View *(1974)*

More Effective Programs for a Cleaner Environment *(1974)*

CED PROFESSIONAL AND ADMINISTRATIVE STAFF

ROBERT C. HOLLAND
President

SOL HURWITZ
Senior Vice President and
  Secretary, Board of Trustees

NATHANIEL M. SEMPLE
Vice President,
  Director of Governmental
  Affairs, and Secretary,
  Research and Policy Committee

PATRICIA O'CONNELL
Vice President and
  Director of Finance

FRANK W. SCHIFF
Vice President
  and Chief Economist

R. SCOTT FOSLER
Vice President and
  Director of Government Studies

ELIZABETH J. LUCIER
Comptroller

KENNETH McLENNAN
Vice President and Director
  of Industrial Studies

CLAUDIA P. FEUREY
Vice President and
  Director of Information

*Advisor on International
Economic Policy*
ISAIAH FRANK
William L. Clayton Professor of
  International Economics
The Johns Hopkins University

Research
SEONG H. PARK
Economist

LORRAINE M. BROOKER
Economic Research Associate

Governmental Affairs
PEGGY MORRISSETTE
Deputy Director
  and Deputy Secretary,
  Research and Policy Committee

Conferences
RUTH MUNSON
Manager

Accounting
CATHERINE F. LEAHY
Deputy Comptroller

Information and Publications
HECTOR GUENTHER
Deputy Director

SANDRA KESSLER HAMBURG
Assistant Director

DEBRA H. KANFER
Publications Manager

Finance
RUTH KALLA
Deputy Director

DOUGLAS A. STAPLES
Associate Director

AMY JEAN O'NEILL
Campaign Coordinator

Administration
THEODORA BOSKOVIC
Administrative Assistant
  to the President

SHIRLEY R. SHERMAN
Administrative Assistant
  to the President

JOHN SULLIVAN WILSON
Assistant to the President

BETTY S. TRIMBLE
Assistant Office Manager

Information Services
TIMOTHY J. MUENCH
Manager

JAMES E. WEBB
Washington, D.C.

GEORGE WEISSMAN, Chairman, Executive
    Committee
Philip Morris Incorporated

WILLIAM H. WENDEL, Vice Chairman
Kennecott Corporation

J. HUBER WETENHALL
New York, New York

GEORGE L. WILCOX, Retired Vice Chairman
Westinghouse Electric Corporation

ARTHUR M. WOOD, Director
Sears, Roebuck and Co.

Honorary Trustees On Leave For Government Service

WILLIAM A. HEWITT
U.S. Ambassador to Jamaica

RESEARCH ADVISORY BOARD

Chairman
THOMAS C. SCHELLING
Professor of Political Economy
John Fitzgerald Kennedy School of Government
Harvard University

RICHARD N. COOPER
Maurits C. Boas Professor of
    International Economics
Harvard University

MARTIN FELDSTEIN
President
National Bureau of Economic Research, Inc.

VICTOR R. FUCHS
Professor of Economics
Stanford University

DONALD HAIDER
Professor and Program Director
J.L. Kellogg Graduate School of Management
Northwestern University

PAUL KRUGMAN
Professor of Economics
Sloan School of Management
Massachusetts Institute of Technology

PAUL W. McCRACKEN
Edmund Ezra Day University Professor
Graduate School of Business Administration
University of Michigan

JACK A. MEYER
Resident Fellow in Economics
American Enterprise Institute for Public Policy Research

DANIEL H. SAKS
Professor of Education Policy and of Economics
Institute for Public Policy Studies
Vanderbilt University

ISABEL V. SAWHILL
Program Director
The Urban Institute

CHARLES L. SCHULTZE
Senior Fellow
The Brookings Institution

CHARLES N. KIMBALL, President Emeritus
Midwest Research Institute

HARRY W. KNIGHT, Chairman of the Board
Hillsboro Associates, Inc.

SIGURD S. LARMON
New York, New York

ELMER L. LINDSETH
Shaker Heights, Ohio

JAMES A. LINEN
Greenwich, Connecticut

GEORGE H. LOVE
Pittsburgh, Pennsylvania

ROBERT A. LOVETT, Partner
Brown Brothers Harriman & Co.

ROY G. LUCKS
San Francisco, California

FRANKLIN J. LUNDING
Sarasota, Florida

RAY W. MacDONALD, Honorary Chairman of the
  Board
Burroughs Corporation

IAN MacGREGOR, Former Chairman
AMAX Inc.

MALCOLM MacNAUGHTON, Chairman, Executive
  Committee
Castle & Cooke, Inc.

FRANK L. MAGEE
Stahlstown, Pennsylvania

G. BARRON MALLORY
New York, New York

STANLEY MARCUS, Consultant
Carter Hawley Hale Stores, Inc.

AUGUSTINE R. MARUSI, Chairman, Executive
  Committee
Borden Inc.

OSCAR G. MAYER, Retired Chairman
Oscar Mayer & Co.

L. F. McCOLLUM
Houston, Texas

JOHN A. McCONE
Pebble Beach, California

GEORGE C. McGHEE, Corporate Director
  and Former U.S. Ambassador
Washington, D.C.

J.W. McSWINEY, Director
The Mead Corporation

CHAUNCEY J. MEDBERRY III, Chairman, Executive
  Committee
Bank of America N.T. & S.A.

JOHN F. MERRIAM
San Francisco, California

LORIMER D. MILTON
Citizens Trust Company

DON G. MITCHELL
Summit, New Jersey

LEE L. MORGAN, Chairman of the Board, Retired
Caterpillar Tractor Co.

ROBERT R. NATHAN, Chairman
Robert R. Nathan Associates, Inc.

ALFRED C. NEAL
Harrison, New York

J. WILSON NEWMAN, Former Chairman of the
  Board
Dun & Bradstreet Corporation

THOMAS O. PAINE, President
Thomas Paine Associates

JOHN H. PERKINS, Former President
Continental Illinois National Bank and Trust Company
  of Chicago

HOWARD C. PETERSEN
Radnor, Pennsylvania

C. WREDE PETERSMEYER
John's Island, Florida

RUDOLPH A. PETERSON, President (Retired)
Bank of America N.T. & S.A.

DONALD C. PLATTEN, Chairman, Executive
  Committee
Chemical Bank

R. STEWART RAUCH, Former Chairman
The Philadelphia Saving Fund Society

PHILIP D. REED
New York, New York

AXEL G. ROSIN, Retired Chairman
Book-of-the-Month Club, Inc.

WILLIAM M. ROTH
San Francisco, California

GEORGE RUSSELL
Bloomfield Hills, Michigan

E. C. SAMMONS, Chairman of the Board (Emeritus)
The United States National Bank of Oregon

CHARLES J. SCANLON
Essex, Connecticut

JOHN A. SCHNEIDER, President
Warner Amex Satellite Entertainment Company

ELLERY SEDGWICK, JR.
Cleveland Heights, Ohio

ROBERT B. SEMPLE, Retired Chairman
BASF Wyandotte Corporation

LEON SHIMKIN, Chairman Emeritus
Simon and Schuster, Inc.

RICHARD R. SHINN, Former Chairman
Metropolitan Life Insurance Company

WILLIAM P. SIMMONS, Chairman
Trust Company of Middle Georgia

NEIL D. SKINNER
Indianapolis, Indiana

ELLIS D. SLATER
Landrum, South Carolina

DONALD B. SMILEY, Chairman, Finance Committee
R. H. Macy & Co., Inc.

DAVIDSON SOMMERS
Washington, D.C.

ROBERT C. SPRAGUE, Honorary Chairman of the
  Board
Sprague Electric Company

ELVIS J. STAHR, JR., Partner
Chickering & Gregory

FRANK STANTON, President Emeritus
CBS Inc.

SYDNEY STEIN, JR., Partner
Stein Roe & Farnham

EDGAR B. STERN, JR., President
Royal Street Corporation

J. PAUL STICHT, Chairman, Executive
  Committee
R. J. Reynolds Industries, Inc.

ALEXANDER L. STOTT
Ponte Vedra, Florida

C. A. TATUM, JR., Chairman
Texas Utilities Company

ALAN H. TEMPLE
New York, New York

WAYNE E. THOMPSON, Chairman
Merritt Peralta Medical Center

CHARLES C. TILLINGHAST, JR.
Providence, Rhode Island

HOWARD S. TURNER, Retired Chairman
Turner Construction Company

ROBERT C. WEAVER
New York, New York

HONORARY TRUSTEES

RAY C. ADAM, Retired Chairman
NL Industries, Inc.
E. SHERMAN ADAMS
New Preston, Connecticut
CARL E. ALLEN
North Muskegon, Michigan
JAMES L. ALLEN, Honorary Chairman
Booz·Allen & Hamilton Inc.
O. KELLEY ANDERSON
Boston, Massachusetts
ROBERT O. ANDERSON, Chairman of the
  Board
Atlantic Richfield Company
SANFORD S. ATWOOD
Lake Toxaway, North Carolina
JOSEPH W. BARR, Corporate Director
Arlington, Virginia
HARRY HOOD BASSETT, Chairman, Executive
  Committee
Southeast Bank N.A.
S. CLARK BEISE, President (Retired)
Bank of America N.T. & S.A.
GEORGE F. BENNETT, President
State Street Research & Management Company
HAROLD H. BENNETT
Salt Lake City, Utah
HOWARD W. BLAUVELT
Charlottesville, Virginia
JOSEPH L. BLOCK, Former Chairman
Inland Steel Company
FRED J. BORCH
New Canaan, Connecticut
MARVIN BOWER, Director
McKinsey & Company, Inc.
R. MANNING BROWN, JR., Director
New York Life Insurance Co., Inc.
JOHN L. BURNS, President
John L. Burns and Company
THOMAS D. CABOT, Honorary Chairman of the
  Board
Cabot Corporation
ALEXANDER CALDER, JR., Chairman, Executive
  Committee
Union Camp Corporation
PHILIP CALDWELL, Senior Managing Director
Shearson Lehman Brothers Inc.
EDWARD W. CARTER, Chairman Emeritus
Carter Hawley Hale Stores, Inc.
EVERETT N. CASE
Van Hornesville, New York
HUNG WO CHING, Chairman of the Board
Aloha Airlines, Inc.
WALKER L. CISLER
Detroit, Michigan
ROBERT C. COSGROVE
Naples, Florida
GEORGE S. CRAFT
Atlanta, Georgia
JOHN P. CUNNINGHAM, Honorary Chairman of the
  Board
Cunningham & Walsh, Inc.
JOHN H. DANIELS, Retired Chairman
National City Bancorporation
ARCHIE K. DAVIS, Chairman of the Board (Retired)
Wachovia Bank and Trust Company, N.A.
DONALD C. DAYTON, Director
Dayton Hudson Corporation
DOUGLAS DILLON, Chairman, Executive Committee
Dillon, Read and Co. Inc.
ALFRED W. EAMES, JR., Retired Chairman
Del Monte Corporation
FRANCIS E. FERGUSON, Retired Chairman
  of the Board
Northwestern Mutual Life Insurance
  Company
JOHN T. FEY, Chairman
The National Westminster Bank USA
WILLIAM S. FISHMAN, Chairman, Executive
  Committee
ARA Services, Inc.
EDMUND FITZGERALD
Milwaukee, Wisconsin
JOHN M. FOX
Orlando, Florida
CLARENCE FRANCIS
New York, New York
GAYLORD FREEMAN
Chicago, Illinois
DON C. FRISBEE, Chairman
PacifiCorp
W. H. KROME GEORGE, Chairman,
  Executive Committee
Aluminum Company of America
PAUL S. GEROT, Honorary Chairman of the
  Board
The Pillsbury Company
LINCOLN GORDON, Guest Scholar
The Brookings Institution
KATHARINE GRAHAM, Chairman
The Washington Post Company
JOHN D. GRAY, Chairman Emeritus
Hartmarx Corp.
WILLIAM C. GREENOUGH, Retired
  Chairman
TIAA and CREF
WALTER A. HAAS, JR., Honorary Chairman
  of the Board
Levi Strauss and Co.
MICHAEL L. HAIDER
New York, New York
TERRANCE HANOLD
Minneapolis, Minnesota
ROBERT S. HATFIELD
New York, New York
H. J. HEINZ II, Chairman
H. J. Heinz Company
J. V. HERD, Director
The Continental Insurance Companies
OVETA CULP HOBBY, Chairman
H&C Communications, Inc.
GEORGE F. JAMES
South Bristol, Maine
HENRY R. JOHNSTON
Ponte Vedra Beach, Florida
GILBERT E. JONES, Retired Vice Chairman
IBM Corporation
FREDERICK R. KAPPEL
Sarasota, Florida
CHARLES KELLER, JR.
New Orleans, Louisiana
DAVID M. KENNEDY
Salt Lake City, Utah
JAMES R. KENNEDY
Essex Fells, New Jersey

BRUCE M. ROCKWELL, Chairman of the Board
Colorado National Bank

IAN M. ROLLAND, Chairman
Lincoln National Life Insurance Company

FRANCIS C. ROONEY, JR., Chairman of the Board
Melville Corporation

DONALD K. ROSS, Chairman of the Board
New York Life Insurance Company

THOMAS F. RUSSELL, Chairman and Chief Executive
    Officer
Federal-Mogul Corporation

JOHN SAGAN, Vice President—Treasurer
Ford Motor Company

RALPH S. SAUL, Chairman of the Board
Peers & Co.

HENRY B. SCHACHT, Chairman of the Board and Chief
    Executive Officer
Cummins Engine Company, Inc.

ROBERT M. SCHAEBERLE, Chairman
Nabisco Brands Inc.

GEORGE A. SCHAEFER, Chairman and Chief Executive
    Officer
Caterpillar Tractor Co.

WILLIAM A. SCHREYER, Chairman and Chief
    Executive Officer
Merrill Lynch & Co. Inc.

DONALD J. SCHUENKE, President and Chief Executive
    Officer
Northwestern Mutual Life Insurance Company

ROBERT G. SCHWARTZ, Chairman of the Board
Metropolitan Life Insurance Company

J. L. SCOTT, Chairman and Chief Executive Officer
J. L. Scott Enterprises, Inc.

S. F. SEGNAR, Chairman, President and Chief Executive
    Officer
InterNorth, Inc.

DONNA E. SHALALA, President
Hunter College

MARK SHEPHERD, JR., Chairman
Texas Instruments Incorporated

WALTER V. SHIPLEY, Chairman and Chief Executive
    Officer
Chemical Bank

ROCCO C. SICILIANO, Chairman, Executive
    Committee
Ticor

ANDREW C. SIGLER, Chairman and Chief Executive
    Officer
Champion International Corporation

RICHARD D. SIMMONS, President
The Washington Post Company

L. EDWIN SMART, Chairman of the Board
Transworld Corporation

FREDERICK W. SMITH, Chairman and Chief Executive
    Officer
Federal Express Corporation

PHILIP L. SMITH, President and Chief Operating
    Officer
General Foods Corporation

RICHARD M. SMITH, Vice Chairman
Bethlehem Steel Corporation

ROGER B. SMITH, Chairman
General Motors Corporation

SHERWOOD H. SMITH, JR., Chairman and President
Carolina Power & Light Company

ELMER B. STAATS, Former Comptroller General of the
    United States
Washington, D.C.

DELBERT C. STALEY, Chairman and Chief Executive
    Officer
NYNEX Corporation

DONALD M. STEWART, President
Spelman College

WILLIAM P. STIRITZ, Chairman of the Board
Ralston Purina Company

*WILLIAM C. STOLK
Bridgeport, Connecticut

ELLEN S. STRAUS, President and General Manager
WMCA Radio

BARRY F. SULLIVAN, Chairman of the Board
First National Bank of Chicago

HOWARD R. SWEARER, President
Brown University

MORRIS TANENBAUM, Executive Vice President
AT&T

G. J. TANKERSLEY, Chairman
Consolidated Natural Gas Company

DAVID S. TAPPAN, JR., Chairman and Chief Executive
    Officer
Fluor Corporation

EDWARD R. TELLING, Chairman of the Board
Sears, Roebuck and Co.

ANTHONY P. TERRACCIANO, Vice Chairman, Global
    Banking
The Chase Manhattan Bank, N.A.

WALTER N. THAYER, Chairman
Whitney Communications Company

W. BRUCE THOMAS, Vice Chairman of
    Administration and Chief Financial Officer
United States Steel Corporation

L. S. TURNER, JR.
Dallas, Texas

THOMAS V. H. VAIL, President, Publisher and Editor
Plain Dealer Publishing Company

THOMAS A. VANDERSLICE, President and Chief
    Executive Officer
Apollo Computer Inc.

HANS W. WANDERS, President
The Wachovia Corporation

ALVA O. WAY, Chairman, Finance Committee
The Travelers Corporation

ARNOLD R. WEBER, President
Northwestern University

SIDNEY J. WEINBERG, JR., Partner
Goldman, Sachs & Co.

WILLIAM L. WEISS, Chairman of the Board
Ameritech

JOHN F. WELCH, JR., Chairman of the Board
General Electric Company

CLIFTON R. WHARTON, JR., Chancellor
State University of New York

ALTON W. WHITEHOUSE, JR., Chairman
The Standard Oil Company (Ohio)

HAROLD M. WILLIAMS, President
The J. Paul Getty Trust

J. KELLEY WILLIAMS, President
First Mississippi Corporation

JOSEPH D. WILLIAMS, Chairman of the Board and
    Chief Executive Officer
Warner-Lambert Company

THOMAS R. WILLIAMS, Chairman and President
First Atlanta Corporation

*W. WALTER WILLIAMS
Seattle, Washington

J. TYLEE WILSON, Chairman and Chief Executive
    Officer
R. J. Reynolds Industries, Inc.

MARGARET S. WILSON, Chairman of the Board
Scarbroughs

RICHARD D. WOOD, Chairman of the Board
Eli Lilly and Company

WILLIAM S. WOODSIDE, Chairman
American Can Company

M. CABELL WOODWARD, JR., Executive Vice
    President and Chief Financial Officer
ITT Corporation

CHARLES J. ZWICK, Chairman and Chief Executive
    Officer
Southeast Banking Corporation

*Life Trustee

LAWRENCE HICKEY, Chairman
Stein Roe & Farnham

RODERICK M. HILLS, Of Counsel
Latham, Watkins & Hills

ROBERT C. HOLLAND, President
Committee for Economic Development

LEON C. HOLT, JR., Vice Chairman and Chief
 Administrative Officer
Air Products and Chemicals, Inc.

ROY M. HUFFINGTON, Chairman of the Board
Roy M. Huffington, Inc.

WILLIAM S. KANAGA, Adviser
Arthur Young

DAVID T. KEARNS, Chairman & Chief Executive Officer
Xerox Corporation

GEORGE M. KELLER, Chairman of the Board
Chevron Corporation

DONALD P. KELLY, President
Kelly Briggs & Associates, Inc.

JAMES M. KEMPER, JR., Chairman of the Board
Commerce Bancshares, Inc.

J. C. KENEFICK, Chairman
Union Pacific System

JAMES L. KETELSEN, Chairman and Chief Executive
 Officer
Tenneco Inc.

TOM KILLEFER, Chairman Emeritus
United States Trust Company of New York

CHARLES M. KITTRELL, Executive Vice President
Phillips Petroleum Company

PHILIP M. KLUTZNICK, Senior Partner
Klutznick Investments

CHARLES F. KNIGHT, Chairman and Chief Executive
 Officer
Emerson Electric Co.

RALPH LAZARUS, Chairman Emeritus
Federated Department Stores, Inc.

DREW LEWIS, Chairman and Chief Executive Officer
Warner Amex Cable Communications

FLOYD W. LEWIS, Chairman and President
Middle South Utilities, Inc.

FRANKLIN A. LINDSAY, Chairman
Vectron, Inc.

HOWARD M. LOVE, Chairman and Chief Executive
 Officer
National Intergroup, Inc.

FRANCIS P. LUCIER, Director
Mohawk Data Sciences Corporation

ROBERT W. LUNDEEN, Chairman of the Board
The Dow Chemical Company

JACK A. MacALLISTER, President and Chief Executive
 Officer
U S WEST, Inc.

BRUCE K. MacLAURY, President
The Brookings Institution

WILLIAM A. MARQUARD, Chairman of the Board
American Standard Inc.

WILLIAM F. MAY, President
Statue of Liberty — Ellis Island Foundation, Inc.

ALONZO L. McDONALD, Chairman and Chief
 Executive Officer
Avenir Group, Inc.

JOHN F. McGILLICUDDY, Chairman of the Board and
 Chief Executive Officer
Manufacturers Hanover Corporation

JAMES W. McKEE, JR., Chairman
CPC International Inc.

JOHN A. McKINNEY, Chairman of the Board and Chief
 Executive Officer
Manville Corporation

CHAMPNEY A. McNAIR, Vice Chairman
Trust Company of Georgia

ROBERT E. MERCER, Chairman of the Board
The Goodyear Tire & Rubber Company

RUBEN F. METTLER, Chairman of the Board and Chief
 Executive Officer
TRW Inc.

RONALD T. MILLER, Chairman
Northwest Natural Gas Company

GEORGE F. MOODY, President and Chief Executive
 Officer
Security Pacific National Bank

STEVEN MULLER, President
The Johns Hopkins University

JOSEPH NEUBAUER, Chairman, President and Chief
 Executive Officer
ARA Services, Inc.

BARBARA W. NEWELL, Lecturer on Education
Harvard University

EDWARD N. NEY, Chairman of the Board
Young & Rubicam Inc.

JAMES J. O'CONNOR, Chairman and President
Commonwealth Edison Company

WILLIAM S. OGDEN, Chairman and Chief Executive
 Officer
Continental Illinois National Bank and Trust
 Company of Chicago

LEIF H. OLSEN, Economic Consultant
Citibank, N.A.

JOHN D. ONG, Chairman of the Board
The BFGoodrich Company

ANTHONY J. F. O'REILLY, President and Chief
 Executive Officer
H. J. Heinz Company

NORMA PACE, Senior Vice President
American Paper Institute

VICTOR H. PALMIERI, Chairman
The Palmieri Company

DANIEL PARKER, Honorary Chairman
The Parker Pen Company

CHARLES W. PARRY, Chairman and Chief Executive
 Officer
Aluminum Company of America

PETER G. PETERSON, Chairman
Peterson, Jacobs & Company

JOHN J. PHELAN, JR., Chairman and Chief Executive
 Officer
New York Stock Exchange, Inc.

DEAN P. PHYPERS, Senior Vice President
IBM Corporation

HAROLD A. POLING, President
Ford Motor Company

EDMUND T. PRATT, JR., Chairman of the Board and
 Chief Executive Officer
Pfizer Inc.

LELAND S. PRUSSIA, Chairman of the Board
Bank of America N.T. & S.A.

JOHN R. PURCELL, Chairman and President
SFN Companies, Inc.

ALLAN L. RAYFIELD, President and Chief Operating
 Officer—Diversified Products and Services Group
GTE Service Corporation

FRANK H. T. RHODES, President
Cornell University

JAMES Q. RIORDAN, Senior Vice President
Mobil Corporation

S. DONLEY RITCHEY, Chairman
Lucky Stores, Inc.

BURNELL R. ROBERTS, Chairman and Chief Executive
 Officer
The Mead Corporation

KENNETH L. ROBERTS, Chairman and Chief Executive
 Officer
First American Corporation

ROBERT F. DEE, Chairman of the Board
SmithKline Beckman Corporation

ROBERT A. dePALMA, Senior Vice President and Chief Financial Officer
Rockwell International Corporation

WILLIAM N. DERAMUS III, Chairman
Kansas City Southern Industries, Inc.

PETER A. DEROW, President
CBS/Publishing Group

JOHN DIEBOLD, Chairman
The Diebold Group, Inc.

GEORGE C. DILLON, Chairman of the Board
Butler Manufacturing Company

ROBERT R. DOCKSON, Chairman of the Board and Chief Executive Officer
California Federal Savings and Loan Association

EDWIN D. DODD, Chairman Emeritus
Owens-Illinois, Inc.

DONALD J. DONAHUE, Retired Chairman
KMI Continental Inc.

JOHN T. DORRANCE, JR., Chairman of the Executive Committee
Campbell Soup Company

JOSEPH P. DOWNER, Vice Chairman of the Board
Atlantic Richfield Company

FRANK P. DOYLE, Senior Vice President
General Electric Company

VIRGINIA A. DWYER, Senior Vice President—Finance
AT&T

W. D. EBERLE, President
Manchester Associates, Ltd.

WILLIAM S. EDGERLY, Chairman of the Board and President
State Street Bank and Trust Company

JOHN R. EDMAN, Vice President
General Motors Corporation

JOHN C. EMERY, JR., Chairman, President and Chief Executive Officer
Emery Air Freight Corporation

ROBERT F. ERBURU, President
The Times Mirror Company

WILLIAM T. ESREY, President and Chief Executive Officer
United Telecommunications, Inc.

J. LEE EVERETT III, Chairman and Chief Executive Officer
Philadelphia Electric Company

LYLE EVERINGHAM, Chairman of the Board and Chief Executive Officer
The Kroger Co.

THOMAS J. EYERMAN, Partner
Skidmore, Owings & Merrill

JAMES B. FARLEY, Senior Chairman
Booz·Allen & Hamilton Inc.

DAVID C. FARRELL, Chairman and Chief Executive Officer
The May Department Stores Company

JOHN H. FILER, Partner
Tyler, Cooper & Alcorn

EDMUND B. FITZGERALD, Chairman and Chief Executive Officer
Northern Telecom Limited

JOSEPH B. FLAVIN, Chairman and Chief Executive Officer
The Singer Company

*WILLIAM H. FRANKLIN, Chairman of the Board, Retired
Caterpillar Tractor Co.

ROBERT E. FRAZER, Chairman
The Dayton Power and Light Company

ROBERT R. FREDERICK, President and Chief Executive Officer
RCA Corporation

HARRY L. FREEMAN, Executive Vice President, Corporate Affairs and Communications
American Express Company

THOMAS F. FRIST, JR., M.D., Chairman and Chief Executive Officer
Hospital Corporation of America

ROBERT F. FROEHLKE, Chairman of the Board
Equitable Life Assurance Society of the United States

GERALD W. FRONTERHOUSE, President and Chief Executive Officer
RepublicBank Corporation

H. LAURANCE FULLER, President
Amoco Corporation

DONALD E. GARRETSON, Community Service Executive Program
3M Company

CLIFTON C. GARVIN, JR., Chairman of the Board
Exxon Corporation

RICHARD L. GELB, Chairman
Bristol-Myers Company

WALTER B. GERKEN, Chairman of the Board
Pacific Mutual Life Insurance Company

PIERRE GOUSSELAND, Chairman of the Board and Chief Executive Officer
AMAX Inc.

THOMAS C. GRAHAM, Vice Chairman and Chief Operating Officer—Steel & Related Resources
United States Steel Corporation

EARL G. GRAVES, President
Earl G. Graves Ltd.

HARRY J. GRAY, Chairman and Chief Executive Officer
United Technologies Corporation

W. GRANT GREGORY, Chairman of the Board
Touche Ross & Co.

DAVID L. GROVE, President
David L. Grove, Ltd.

DONALD E. GUINN, Chairman and Chief Executive Officer
Pacific Telesis Group

JOHN H. GUTFREUND, Chairman and Chief Executive Officer
Phibro-Salomon Inc.

RICHARD P. HAMILTON, Chairman, President, and Chief Executive Officer
Hartmarx Corp.

RICHARD W. HANSELMAN, Chairman, President and Chief Executive Officer
Genesco Inc.

ROBERT A. HANSON, Chairman and Chief Executive Officer
Deere & Company

PAUL HARDIN, President
Drew University

CHARLES M. HARPER, Chairman of the Board and Chief Executive Officer
ConAgra, Inc.

FRED L. HARTLEY, Chairman and President
Unocal Corporation

BARBARA B. HAUPTFUHRER, Corporate Director
Huntingdon Valley, Pennsylvania

ARTHUR HAUSPURG, Chairman of the Board
Consolidated Edison Company of New York, Inc.

PHILIP M. HAWLEY, Chairman of the Board
Carter Hawley Hale Stores, Inc.

RAYMOND A. HAY, Chairman of the Board and Chief Executive Officer
The LTV Corporation

HAROLD W. HAYNES, Executive Vice President and Chief Financial Officer
The Boeing Company

RALPH L. HENNEBACH, Chairman
ASARCO Incorporated

CED BOARD OF TRUSTEES

Chairman
EDMUND B. FITZGERALD, Chairman and Chief
 Executive Officer
Northern Telecom Limited

Vice Chairmen
OWEN B. BUTLER, Chairman of the Board
The Procter & Gamble Company
WILLIAM S. EDGERLY, Chairman of the Board and
 President
State Street Bank and Trust Company
PHILIP M. HAWLEY, Chairman of the Board
Carter Hawley Hale Stores, Inc.
JAMES L. KETELSEN, Chairman and Chief Executive
 Officer
Tenneco Inc.
FRANKLIN A. LINDSAY, Chairman
Vectron, Inc.

Treasurer
JOHN B. CAVE, Executive Vice President—
 Finance
McGraw-Hill, Inc.

EDWARD L. ADDISON, President
The Southern Company
HOWARD P. ALLEN, Chairman and Chief Executive
 Officer
Southern California Edison Company
ROY L. ASH
Los Angeles, California
H. B. ATWATER, JR., Chairman of the Board and Chief
 Executive Officer
General Mills, Inc.
RALPH E. BAILEY, Chairman and Chief Executive
 Officer
Conoco Inc.
ROBERT H. B. BALDWIN, Chairman, Advisory Board
Morgan Stanley & Co. Incorporated
NORMAN BARKER, JR., Chairman of the Board
First Interstate Bank of California
J. DAVID BARNES, Chairman and Chief Executive
 Officer
Mellon Bank N.A.
Z. E. BARNES, Chairman and Chief Executive Officer
Southwestern Bell Corporation
WARREN L. BATTS, President
Dart & Kraft, Inc.
ROBERT A. BECK, Chairman and Chief Executive
 Officer
The Prudential Insurance Company of America
PHILIP E. BEEKMAN, President
Joseph E. Seagram & Sons, Inc.
JACK F. BENNETT, Senior Vice President
Exxon Corporation
JAMES F. BERÉ, Chairman and Chief Executive Officer
Borg-Warner Corporation
DEREK C. BOK, President
Harvard University
JOAN T. BOK, Chairman
New England Electric System
THOMAS E. BOLGER, Chairman of the Board and
 Chief Executive Officer
Bell Atlantic Corporation
ALAN S. BOYD, Chairman
Airbus Industrie of North America

WILLIAM H. BRICKER, Chairman and Chief Executive
 Officer
Diamond Shamrock Corporation
ANDREW F. BRIMMER, President
Brimmer & Company, Inc.
ALFRED BRITTAIN III, Chairman of the Board
Bankers Trust Company
PERRY G. BRITTAIN, Chairman of the Board and
 Chief Executive Officer
Texas Utilities Company
CEES BRUYNES, Chairman, President and Chief
 Executive Officer
North American Philips Corporation
JOHN H. BRYAN, JR., Chairman and Chief Executive
 Officer
Sara Lee Corporation
THEODORE A. BURTIS, Chairman of the Board
Sun Company, Inc.
OWEN B. BUTLER, Chairman of the Board
The Procter & Gamble Company
*FLETCHER L. BYROM, Retired Chairman
Koppers Company, Inc.
ROBERT J. CARLSON, Chairman, President and Chief
 Executive Officer
BMC Industries Inc.
RAFAEL CARRION, JR., Chairman of the Board
Banco Popular de Puerto Rico
R. E. CARTLEDGE, President
Union Camp Corporation
JOHN B. CAVE, Executive Vice President—
 Finance
McGraw-Hill, Inc.
HUGH M. CHAPMAN, Chairman of the Board
Citizens & Southern National Bank of South Carolina
ROBERT A. CHARPIE, President
Cabot Corporation
ROBERT CIZIK, Chairman and President
Cooper Industries, Inc.
DAVID R. CLARE, President
Johnson & Johnson
DONALD C. CLARK, Chairman of the Board and Chief
 Executive Officer
Household International
ROBERT B. CLAYTOR, Chairman and Chief Executive
 Officer
Norfolk Southern Corporation
W. GRAHAM CLAYTOR, JR., Chairman and President
Amtrak
JOHN L. CLENDENIN, Chairman of the Board
BellSouth Corporation
*EMILIO G. COLLADO, Executive Chairman
International Planning Corporation
DOUGLAS D. DANFORTH, Chairman
Westinghouse Electric Corporation
D. RONALD DANIEL, Managing Director
McKinsey & Company, Inc.
RONALD R. DAVENPORT, Chairman of the Board
Sheridan Broadcasting Corporation
RALPH P. DAVIDSON, Chairman of the Board
Time Inc.
BARBARA K. DEBS, Corporate Director
Greenwich, Connecticut
ALFRED C. DeCRANE, JR., President
Texaco Inc.

OBJECTIVES OF THE COMMITTEE FOR ECONOMIC DEVELOPMENT

For over forty years, the Committee for Economic Development has been a respected influence on the formation of business and public policy. CED is devoted to these two objectives:

To develop, through objective research and informed discussion, findings and recommendations for private and public policy that will contribute to preserving and strengthening our free society, achieving steady economic growth at high employment and reasonably stable prices, increasing productivity and living standards, providing greater and more equal opportunity for every citizen, and improving the quality of life for all.

To bring about increasing understanding by present and future leaders in business, government, and education, and among concerned citizens, of the importance of these objectives and the ways in which they can be achieved.

CED's work is supported strictly by private voluntary contributions from business and industry, foundations, and individuals. It is independent, nonprofit, nonpartisan, and nonpolitical.

The two hundred trustees, who generally are presidents or board chairmen of corporations and presidents of universities, are chosen for their individual capacities rather than as representatives of any particular interests. By working with scholars, they unite business judgment and experience with scholarship in analyzing the issues and developing recommendations to resolve the economic problems that constantly arise in a dynamic and democratic society.

Through this business-academic partnership, CED endeavors to develop policy statements and other research materials that commend themselves as guides to public and business policy; that can be used as texts in college economics and political science courses and in management training courses; that will be considered and discussed by newspaper and magazine editors, columnists, and commentators; and that are distributed abroad to promote better understanding of the American economic system.

CED believes that by enabling businessmen to demonstrate constructively their concern for the general welfare, it is helping business to earn and maintain the national and community respect essential to the successful functioning of the free enterprise capitalist system.

Page 11, at the end of the first full paragraph:

"Since World War II, capital investment and economic growth in this country have lagged behind most if not all of the major industrial nations abroad -- all of which are competitors in the American marketplace as well as in markets abroad. Throughout most of this period, capital cost recovery provisions in our country's tax laws have been far less favorable than those abroad, and this situation has contributed materially to the much slower rate with which this nation's plant and equipment have been replaced and upgraded.

"Since the Administration is committed to a policy of free trade, it is imperative that the nation's tax policies with respect to capital investment make our nation's industries (and their employees) viable competitors. Tax laws cannot be considered in a vacuum which ignores competition. To do so would mean that American markets will be swamped with foreign goods, and markets abroad will also become less and less available to us. Unfortunately, elimination of the investment tax credit and replacement of ACRS with CCRS would indeed make our nation much less competitive, our producers less productive, and our employees less employed.

"Economic history here and abroad has shown that everyone benefits from a larger economic pie, that such a pie is brought about by plant and equipment spending, and that capital cost recovery provisions in the tax law materially affect the level of such spending. This is why it would be extremely undesirable to make capital spending far less attractive, as the Administration's proposal would do."

JAMES Q. RIORDAN has asked to be associated with the following footnote:

Page 16, at the end of the third paragraph, following "...approaches:":

"While 'revenue neutrality' is an understandable and desirable objective of the overall tax proposal, there would probably be less drag on economic activity if the objective were 'deficit neutral'. That is, rather than off-setting tax reductions to be realized by individuals with such large tax increases on corporations (particularly through higher taxes on investment in plant and equipment), it would be preferable to cover at least part of the revenue shortfall by reduced government spending. This approach would avoid losing the job-creating and income-producing effects of the higher level of capital investment which is sorely needed to foster economic growth and higher standards of living for the nation."

The following footnote has been submitted by WILLIAM S. WOODSIDE.

Page 2, at the end of the second sentence of the second full paragraph:

"I object to the elimination of the individual deduction for state and local income and property taxes. This proposed change in the tax law should have been specifically rejected in the policy statement because of its drastic impact on the relationships between the federal and various state governments. If enacted into the tax reform proposal, the elimination of the deduction will have serious adverse consequences on the willingness and ability of state and local governments to meet the educational and other obligations which should be provided to their residents."

flaw in today's tax code of not putting all incomes on a common footing for tax purposes.

"The second suggestion with which I differ is the proposal to phase in the planned reductions in tax rates over some number of years and that all new 'add-on' types of taxes be explored. These steps would address the deficit only through raising the level of Federal revenue. I believe that they would diminish the effects of tax reform and that further restraint on Federal outlays is preferable."

The following footnotes have been submitted by ELMER B. STAATS.

ROBERT R. NATHAN has asked to be associated with the following footnote:

Page 1, at the end of the first sentence of the second paragraph:

"I believe the statement should have gone further to deal with the question of priority of further actions to deal with the Federal deficit and the enactment of tax reform legislation. I believe it highly unwise to enact comprehensive tax reform legislation prior to substantial and assured further reductions in the deficit. In spite of the hard-won steps taken by Congress in connection with the current budget resolution, we still face huge deficits for the next several years at least.

"It seems abundantly clear to me as a long-time participant in the budget process that substantial reductions in the deficit cannot be achieved without new sources of revenue. This view is shared by an increasing number of individuals in and out of government. The nature and scope of new revenue legislation should be agreed upon in advance of substantive changes in tax rates which are now proposed by the Administration.

"Final action on tax reform could make the task of enacting new revenue legislation immeasurably more difficult. In a real sense, we run the danger of 'getting the cart before the horse.'"

ROBERT R. NATHAN has asked to be associated with the following footnote:

Page 5, at the end of the second sentence under "Primary Purpose:" and
Page 7, at the end of the first sentence, following "...conflict.":

"In the CED report, Strengthening the Federal Budget Process: A Requirement for Effective Fiscal Control, the CED took the position '...we believe that it would be highly desirable if individual tax expenditure programs and regular spending programs that serve a similar purpose were subjected to joint reviews wherever feasible.' I would have liked to have seen this statement repeated in connection with the discussion of tax expenditures here. While a review of all tax expenditure programs to reduce them to a minimum would undoubtedly be desirable, the real concern which I have is that tax expenditures and direct expenditures for the same or similar programs are not adequately reviewed jointly in the budget process, although the budget committees have increasingly turned their attention to the role of tax expenditures."

The following footnotes have been submitted by W. BRUCE THOMAS.

ROBERT R. NATHAN, CHARLES W. PARRY, and JAMES Q. RIORDAN have asked to be associated with the following footnote:

wish to keep total tax revenues neutral. We should be working on a consumption tax now."

CHARLES W. PARRY and W. BRUCE THOMAS have asked to be associated with the following footnote:

Page 16, at the end of the underlined section:

"The practical possibility that we can raise significant additional revenue from so-called 'base broadening' that would not hurt the economy is illusory. The Statement contains no specific suggestions of base broadening in the corporate area that would be consistent with our Objectives and Principles. There may be some potential in the individual area but if we need significant additional revenue we will need to consider a consumption tax."

CHARLES W. PARRY and W. BRUCE THOMAS have asked to be associated with the following footnote:

Page 18, at the end of the first sentence, following "...in the future.":

"The Statement indicates that more taxes might need to be raised to cope with large budget deficits, i.e. that revenue neutrality may not be enough. This is an unfortunate invitation. Large deficits have not been caused by inadequate taxation. We are now collecting approximately 19 percent of gross national product in federal taxes. We have never collected much more than that and in years past we often collected less. To attempt to collect more would be self-defeating. The deficit problem is a spending problem. Government spending must be reduced to not more than 19 percent of gross national product in years of reasonably full employment."

The following footnote has been submitted by ROGER B. SMITH, with which JAMES L. KETELSEN and CHARLES W. PARRY have asked to be associated.

Page 4, at the end of the first paragraph, following "...neutrality.":

"I do not fully support the CED statement on tax reform. I do agree with the three recommendations that the depreciation windfall recapture provision not be enacted, that care be taken with respect to the overall tax burden falling upon capital as a result of eliminating ITC and modifying depreciation rules, and that taxation of overseas income retain the present overall computations rather than the proposed country-by-country computations. I also share the concern expressed in the statement that nothing be done which would worsen the deficits now built into the federal sector.

"I believe that two aims of tax reform must remain foremost if we are to achieve a tax code that is as equitable and undistorting of economic choices as is possible. The two aims must be to broaden the base of taxable income to minimize different treatments for different kinds of income, and then to set as low as practicable tax rates which apply evenly to all sources of income. Two specific suggestions in the statement run counter to these aims.

"One of the CED suggestions with which I disagree is to single out investment in equipment for special treatment. The suggestion that a tax treatment close to full expensing should be explored for equipment comes very close to exempting returns to investment in equipment from taxation. This would force increased burdens upon other types of income, exacerbating the key

"1) The Committee supports proposals to lower marginal rates, establish the principle of not taxing dividends twice, and introduce an inflation factor into future depreciation schedules.

"2) The Statement opposes changes that would make the capital recovery provisions more onerous than current law and recommends that the current treatment of foreign income be left unchanged.

"3) The Committee deliberately did not address proposals that were thought to have primary importance to particular industries or states. Thus it did not decide whether the proposed changes regarding capital gains, fringe benefits or deductibility of state and local taxes were good or bad or whether the proposed new rules for the timber, insurance and banking industries were good or bad.

"4) The Statement also comments favorably on other unspecified aspects of the President's proposal because 'it reduces some of the disparities in effective tax rates paid on the same type of income' and 'it eliminates a number of nonproductive preferences.' In light of other positions that the Statement takes and does not take it is not clear to me what other significant proposals are being supported."

CHARLES W. PARRY and W. BRUCE THOMAS have asked to be associated with the following footnote:

Page 9, at the end of the first sentence under the heading "Concerns about Treatment of Investment":

"This is the strongest section of the Statement. It clearly reaffirms our opposition to revisions to the tax law that would inhibit productive investment or damage the international competitiveness of U.S. business. The Statement implies that we would be better off with current law unless the provisions that adversely affected investment and international competitiveness are eliminated. I think this section would have been even better if we had stated that conclusion more clearly."

CHARLES W. PARRY has asked to be associated with the following footnote:

Page 15, at the end of the first sentence under the heading "Making Up Revenue Shortfalls":

"The commentary beginning here properly reemphasizes CED's concern with the deficit. The Statement takes the position that any changes in the income tax law should be revenue neutral. Consistent with that position it recommends a phasing-in of the proposed reductions in corporate and individual rates to cover revenue losses that might arise from our capital recovery and international competitiveness recommendations.

"The Statement also assumes, however, that Congress can achieve rate reduction, dividend deduction, take the poor off the tax rolls, maintain the research and development credit, maintain appropriate capital investment and international competitiveness provisions and still come up with a revenue neutral income tax package. It is for this reason that the Statement concludes that we can defer consideration of a consumption tax. I disagree with the assumption and the conclusion. We will need to enact a consumption tax at the same time we lower income tax rates and increase exemptions if we

ROBERT B. NATHAN, JAMES Q. RIORDAN, and W. BRUCE THOMAS have asked to be associated with the following footnote:

Page 10, at the end of the first full paragraph:

"I urge the retention of the current accelerated depreciation system along with some realistic amount of investment tax credit. We do not have to devise exotic alternatives to these straight-forward capital incentives under current law. They have proved vital to the expansion of American business and the creation of new jobs (or maintenance of existing jobs). To date, most of the proposals with respect to basic industry have overlooked the fact that our current capital formation tax system ranks amongst the most competitive in the world. Those proposals which would remove these existing incentives will result in putting American industry at the bottom of such world ranking."

ROBERT R. NATHAN, JAMES Q. RIORDAN and W. BRUCE THOMAS have asked to be associated with the following footnote:

Page 17, at the end of the underlined section:

"I would urge that we still continue to consider as a viable option a phase-in of all tax rate reductions (or even less generous rate changes). I cannot emphasize too strongly that the health of basic industry should not be sacrificed on the altar of tax rate reduction."

JAMES Q. RIORDAN and W. BRUCE THOMAS have asked to be associated with the following footnote:

Page 18, at the end of the second paragraph:

"We may be forced into exploring various revenue alternatives as pointed out here. If and when that happens, I would urge that any such additional revenue devices be legally conditioned on targeted reduction in federal spending."

The following footnotes have been submitted by JAMES Q. RIORDAN.

CHARLES W. PARRY and W. BRUCE THOMAS have asked to be associated with the following footnote:

Page 3, at the end of the first sentence of the second full paragraph:

"The U.S. tax system should be reformed in accordance with the Objectives and Principles set forth in the Statement. Both the Objectives and Principles and our earlier statements make clear the importance of not ldversely affecting savings, investment and U.S. international competitiveness. We should not be satisfied with a revised tax system that 'would have no more detrimental effect on productive investment than the present system.' The present system is biased in favor of consumption and against savings and investment. That bias should be reduced in accordance with our Objectives and Principles."

CHARLES W. PARRY has asked to be associated with the following footnote:

Page 7, at the end of the first sentence of the first full paragraph:

Page 4, following the third bullet:

"The issue of equity and fairness is central to any tax system and that does require the same treatment for taxpayers in comparable circumstances. But it also requires different treatment of taxpayers in different circumstances. The principle of 'ability to pay' as a determinant in tax policies has a long history in the United States. It should be reiterated and supported explicitly in a program of tax reform."

W. BRUCE THOMAS has asked to be associated with the following footnote:

Page 5, at the end of the first sentence under "Primary Purpose":

"Of course, the principal goal of taxation is revenue. However, many essential and desirable government policies can be more economically achieved by taxes or tax credits than by regulations or subsidies or government ownership and operation. In fact, regulation and subsidization may be more complex and more disruptive than tax measures to attain desirable policies such as high levels of private investment."

W. BRUCE THOMAS has asked to be associated with the following footnote:

Page 18, at the end of the second paragraph:

"On this point I register a strong dissent. In 1981 income taxes were reduced 25 percent over a three year period. Now it is proposed, by tax reform, again to lower income tax rates substantially. To avoid revenue losses from tax reforms or meet the needs for added revenues in the near future (as is so clearly essential) reductions in income tax rates should be less than proposed or phased in gradually rather than resorting to 'a consumption-tax approach.' All will agree that more intensive studies of revenue options are needed and should be undertaken. But, for dealing with the huge budget deficits promptly and with revenue losses attributable to tax reform, income tax rates provide the appropriate vehicle rather than pursuing new sources of revenue which will further delay urgently needed action to reduce the budget deficits."

The following footnotes have been submitted by CHARLES W. PARRY.

JAMES Q. RIORDAN and W. BRUCE THOMAS have asked to be associated with the following footnote:

Page 4, line 6, following "...will have to be minimized.":

"The approaches taken so far on the tax reform effort have been fundamentally flawed by seeking to pay for beneficial rate reduction by a massive shift of tax burden on certain segments of American business. Unless this approach is changed much of our basic industry will be unable to effectively compete in the world marketplace. The resulting loss of markets will lead inevitably to the loss of U.S. jobs. If that occurs, we will have constructed a fairer tax system only to find that many of the beneficiaries cannot enjoy it because they have lost their jobs."

The following footnote has been submitted by <u>PHILIP M. KLUTZNICK</u>.

<u>Page 5</u>, at the end of the second sentence under the "Accountability" heading:

"I believe this worthy principle is needed to help check not only politicians, but many different participants in the political process."

The following footnote has been submitted by <u>WILLIAM F. MAY</u>, with which W. BRUCE THOMAS has asked to be associated.

<u>Page 1</u>, at the end of the first sentence of the second paragraph:

"Balancing the budget may require extension of the current tax base and may also necessitate a deviation from the excellent principle of a revenue-neutral tax reform."

The following footnotes have been submitted by <u>ROBERT R. NATHAN</u>.

<u>Page 1</u>, at the end of the first sentence of the second paragraph:

"Every serious observer of the American economic scene will agree that United States budget deficits reflect an economic crisis of disastrous proportions. The CED commendably urged aggressive measures (including revenues), to reduce the deficits.

"The 'revenue neutral' tax reform program inevitably precluded major progress toward lower deficits. Either increased revenues should have been given priority over tax reform or the tax reform proposals should have been designed to achieve both reform and higher revenues.

"As bitter as the battle has been and continues to be over the President's dubious tax reform proposals, even more divisive will be the ensuing struggle to increase revenues if tax reform measures are passed. Tax reformers can be expected to argue that having reformed income taxes it would be highly inappropriate to raise income tax rates to get more revenue. Therefore the suggested solution will be to resort to sales taxes or value-added taxes. Any income tax reforms enacted will certainly not be of sufficient economic value to warrant such a regressive revenue solution to the budget deficit crisis."

<u>Page 3</u>, at the end of the first sentence:

"This statement properly recognizes the need for increased levels of investment if we are to improve our productivity and strengthen our competitiveness in international markets. We need the investment tax credit and accelerated depreciation to stimulate investment. Also, it would be desirable to have lower corporate income tax rates. However, in the context of the unprecedented and damaging budget deficits the combination of both lower corporation rates and retained incentives is not warranted. This report makes some suggestions for preventing this combination from increasing deficits, but these may well prove to be not supportable and unattainable."

Page 7, at the end of the first paragraph, following "...maximum extent feasible.":

"The CED policy statement on tax reform begins on a very high plane. It identifies a set of desirable objectives and principles of tax reform. It lends support to tax code revisions that give the marketplace a broader role in directing resource use. And it highlights, once again, the critical importance of dealing with the unacceptably large Federal deficit, both within and outside the context of tax reform. For these reasons alone, its publication should make a contribution to the growing debate on this topic.

"Unfortunately however, the statement (like much of the debate on this topic) falls short of delivering an internally consistent position based on its own tax reform objectives. While the CED statement initially appears to favor a tax code that minimizes the impact of tax considerations on economic decision-making, it goes on to recommend one that tilts such decisions toward spending in one area (i.e. industrial investment).

"The implied desire to 'have it both ways' is not unique to the CED. But, from this body, it is nevertheless unfortunate. For every sacred cow that gets protected in the current tax code, another opportunity for broader marketplace involvement in economic decisions will be lost.

"While econometric modeling is a valuable analytical tool, it would be a mistake for us to make fundamental, long-term tax policy decisions on the implied results from such studies. Such studies are far from precise. It cannot be otherwise. When assumed conditions change (as they surely will), so will the results. Ultimately, that has to be the strongest argument for tax code revisions that expand marketplace involvement in economic decision-making."

The following footnote has been submitted by THOMAS J. EYERMAN.

Page 10, at the end of the first full paragraph:

"I firmly believe that CED is an institution which should assert moral and intellectual leadership in the business community specifically, and in the public at large generally. Often the demonstration of leadership requires a sacrifice of some perceived personal interest for the larger common good. At the outset, the policy statement recognizes that there 'is a clear need for basic tax reform to make the U.S. tax structure significantly simpler and fairer, as well as more conducive to economic efficiency, sound economic growth, and U.S. international competitiveness.' Despite this recognition of the necessity of tax reform, the statement then goes on to argue why the key current tax provisions that benefit a large number of industrial corporations should be retained. It seems to me that it is inconsistent to argue for major meaningful tax reform while at the same time arguing for depreciation schedules which are tantamount to expensing and for retention of the investment tax credit in its current or even modified form.

"Since I personally favor tax reform, I am unable to support our policy statement."

The following footnote has been submitted by FRANK P. DOYLE, with which W. BRUCE THOMAS has asked to be associated.

Page 10, at the end of the first full paragraph:

"My concerns about the adverse impact of certain Administration proposals on investment and international competitiveness extend to proposals for a 'high rate' minimum tax which would treat as tax preferences R&D expenditures in excess of straight-line amortization and the excess of accelerated depreciation over nonaccelerated depreciation on machinery and equipment. Such a minimum tax would sharply curtail R&D activities and investment in productive assets essential to the innovation process -- the key to international competitiveness, economic growth and job creation. The result would be to make U.S.-made products less competitive in domestic and foreign markets, endanger U.S. industry's technological leadership, widen the trade deficit and encourage the export of jobs. To avoid such dire results, any minimum tax that may be enacted should not treat R&D expenditures and accelerated depreciation on machinery and equipment as preferences. Moreover, to reduce the punitive nature of such a tax, the minimum tax rate should not be greater than one-half of the regular corporate tax rate or, in the case of individuals, one-half the regular tax rates, using the same brackets."

The following footnotes have been submitted by LYLE EVERINGHAM.

Page 2, at the end of the last sentence of the page:

"There is no doubt, of course, that many of the features in the current tax code help encourage capital investment. Other things being equal, the modifications suggested in the Administration's tax reform proposal would tend to reduce such investments. However, other things are not being held equal by the proposal. The proposed significant reductions in _marginal_ tax rates would give both consumers and corporations considerably more freedom to follow _market signals_ as they make purchase and investment decisions.

"I agree, of course, that the industrial sector of our economy has been especially hard hit by the emergence of a huge foreign trade deficit and widespread job losses. I do not agree, however, that tax policy is the appropriate place to deal with such problems. If it is necessary to subsidize capital formation in such industries, it should be done openly and directly. The tax code should not be used as an imperfect substitute for a national 'industrial policy.'

"Policy changes as dramatic as those proposed by the Administration's tax reform proposal always impose some costs, partly because they create considerable uncertainty. For that reason alone, it is important to articulate the investment concerns highlighted in the CED paper and to provide for a responsible transition. It is, however, regrettable that CED's position does not represent a deeper underlying faith in the marketplace as an allocator of the nation's resources."

MEMORANDA OF COMMENT, RESERVATION, OR DISSENT

The following footnote has been submitted by <u>RALPH E. BAILEY</u>, with which <u>JAMES Q. RIORDAN</u>, and <u>W. BRUCE THOMAS</u> have asked to be associated.

<u>Page 7</u>, at the end of the first sentence of the first full paragraph:

"Numerous economic analyses, performed by corporate staffs and by major econometric forecasting firms, indicate that the President's tax reform proposal would reduce business fixed investment, especially in equipment. This reduction in investment would slow the introduction of new technology, retard productivity growth, and diminish the ability of American companies to compete in international markets. It is my view that such adverse impacts constitute significant departures from CED tax reform objectives. Specifically, three CED principles are violated: long-run stability, economic efficiency, and improvements in the international competitiveness of the U.S. economy. I believe that the inability of tax reform proposals to date to satisfy these three principles suggests that, despite good faith efforts by all concerned, the present debate on tax reform is unlikely to have a result truly beneficial to the nation. A successful effort to lessen the distorting influences of the federal budget deficit and the deepening U.S. trade imbalance appears to be a prerequisite to the type of tax reform that would achieve the outcome desired by the CED. Therefore, I cannot support either an explicit or implicit CED endorsement of the present Reagan Administration proposal on tax reform."

The following footnote has been submitted by <u>JACK F. BENNETT</u>, with which <u>EMILIO G. COLLADO, CHARLES W. PARRY, JAMES Q. RIORDAN</u>, and <u>W. BRUCE THOMAS</u> have asked to be associated.

<u>Page 3</u>, at the end of the first sentence of the second full paragraph:

"While it is useful for the statement to urge that tax reform not be more detrimental to productive investment than present law, I regret that the statement does not point out forcefully that present law <u>is</u> <u>now</u> damaging the economy by imposing on average a discriminatory high burden of taxation on income earned through investment in corporate operations. And it is unfortunate that, because of the time the statement was drafted, it could not stress how much more detrimental would be the proposals recently recommended by the staff to the House Ways and Means Committee. Those unprincipled proposals would not only seriously delay recognition of depreciation, but would eliminate completely the acknowledgement in the administration's proposals that some inflation-indexing of capital receipts is necessary to prevent the application of income taxes to what is really not income. Those proposals would, moreover, all but eliminate the small step proposed by the administration to reduce the double taxation of income earned through corporate investment."

We recognize, however, that greater revenue needs might arise in the future.* Large budget deficits remain to be dealt with. Primary emphasis should be on further federal expenditure restraints, but even stringent efforts to curtail spending may leave some portion of future deficits to be covered by revenue increases. In addition, the Administration tax reform proposal, and also our recommended revisions, could entail significant revenue losses after the first five years.

In view of these possibilities, we believe there is need to explore a wider range of revenue options. In particular, we urge more intensive study by both government and the private sector of the possible use of add-on taxes -- especially including consumption taxes -- to raise revenue if needed.**

As a contribution to the public dialogue on pros and cons of using alternative forms of taxation, CED has sponsored preparation of a monograph by Professor David Bradford of Princeton University on Untangling the Income Tax that will be published by Harvard University Press early next year.*** We plan to devote continuing attention to these alternatives in the year ahead.

---

*See memorandum by JAMES Q. RIORDAN (page 26).
*See memoranda by ROBERT R. NATHAN (page 23) and CHARLES W. PARRY (page 24).
***If you are interested in obtaining copies of Untangling the Income Tax upon publication, please contact:

   Distribution Department
   Committee for Economic Development/Division C
   477 Madison Avenue
   New York, NY 10022

<u>Second, to the extent that overall revenue neutrality cannot be achieved by further base-broadening alone, we recommend an appropriate phasing-in of the proposed reductions in corporate and individual tax rates.</u>*

It has been estimated that for individuals, each one percentage point increase in tax rates above the 15, 25 and 35 percent rates proposed in the Administration's plan would increase revenues by roughly $20 billion a year. Each one percentage point increase in corporate tax rates above the proposed 33 percent rate would yield approximately $2.5 billion a year. Given these magnitudes, any phasing-in of rates that may be required to offset the 1986-1990 revenue effects of our suggested modifications of the plan would imply only relatively small and temporary changes from the schedule of rate reductions contained in the President's proposal. This should especially be the case if -- as we believe is highly desirable -- any lessening in the marginal rate reductions proposed by the President is considered only after full consideration of the potential for additional base-broadening.

The preceding discussion has not dealt with the case for raising additional revenue through a new across-the-board "overlay" or "add-on" tax, either within an income tax framework or along a consumption-tax approach (e.g., a value-added or other transactions tax). For the reasons just outlined, rendering our proposals revenue-neutral for the next five years would probably not require raising enough additional net revenue to make worthwhile all the efforts, complexity, and time it would take to develop and introduce a wholly new form of taxation.

---

*See memorandum by CHARLES W. PARRY (page 24).

In sum, a five-year total of about $120 to $140 billion would have to be raised to compensate for the revenue effects of our suggested changes in the Administration's proposal.

Since definitive information regarding the likely revenue losses induced by the Administration's tax reform plan subsequent to FY 1990 is not yet available, we have not attempted to estimate the revenue offsets that would be needed to achieve revenue neutrality over the longer term if our proposed modifications of the President's proposals were adopted. However, we believe that a viable tax reform proposal must make adequate provisions to assure that the proposal will not result in long-term revenue losses.

In our view, the methods used to generate the additional revenue needed to produce a revenue-neutral overall tax reform proposal should be designed to avoid an overburdening of investment relative to consumption. With this in mind, we recommend that the effort to raise the additional revenue needed over the next five years focus on the following approaches:*

<u>First, every effort should be made to raise the required revenue through further base-broadening, along lines that are consistent with the tax reform principles set forth earlier in this statement.</u>** Such base-broadening is a particularly desirable way to raise additional revenue because it would not involve increases in the proposed marginal tax rates.

---

*See memorandum by W. BRUCE THOMAS (page 28).
**See memorandum by JAMES Q. RIORDAN (page 26).

and complex. <u>Hence, we feel that changes in the existing rules regarding the allocation of income and expense between U.S. and foreign sources should not be considered without extensive further study and ought not be included in the current tax reform effort.</u>

Making Up Revenue Shortfalls

We believe it is absolutely essential that tax reform not result in any net revenue loss that would add to the budget deficit.*

Offsetting revenue increases would clearly be required to compensate for the revenue losses implied by the existing version of the Administration's proposal and by our specific recommendations for improvements. For the FY 1986-FY 1990 period, the cumulative revenue increases needed to compensate for revenue shortfalls implied by our recommendations include, in particular:

- Nearly $60 billion in corporate and individual receipts over four years to compensate for our proposal to eliminate the provision for a recapture tax.

- Perhaps $50 to $70 billion to shift to a depreciation schedule that is more favorable to investment than the Administration's proposal, along the lines indicated earlier.[10]

- Roughly $10 billion over five years to retain the overall limitation on the foreign tax credit.

---

10. Since our proposed change in the depreciation schedules under the Administration's plan would in effect restore the cost-reducing benefits of the Investment Tax Credit, the above numbers make no allowance for the cost of a "binding contract rule" to ease the phaseout from the Investment Tax Credit. Should our proposal not be adopted, however, provision for such a rule would clearly be appropriate. The cumulative cost of instituting such a rule would come to about $8 billion.

*See memorandum by JAMES Q. RIORDAN (page 25).

overall limitation method of computing the foreign tax credit or some equivalent thereof. Furthermore, as the Administration itself has conceded, the proposed change would create very substantial additional complexities for foreign tax administration, compliance, and enforcement.[8] <u>We therefore recommend that the present overall limitation method of computing the foreign tax credit be retained.</u>

The Administration's proposals also call for various changes in the current rules for determining whether items of income or expense are from a U.S. source or a foreign source for purposes of calculating the foreign tax credit. These rules include those relating to the allocation of interest expense and of export sales income by U.S. multinational corporations. The proposals would also effectively abrogate the current rules regarding allocation of research and development expenses between U.S. and foreign sources by failing to call for an extension of current legislative authority for such rules. Without such an extension, these rules would expire by the end of 1985.[9]

The currently effective rules in these areas have been in place for years. Changes in these rules are likely to have significant adverse effects on the competitive position of U.S. firms engaged in international operations, at a time when competitive pressures are intense. The issues involved in making such changes are highly technical

---

8. A special task force of the House Ways and Means Committee which studied the relative merits of the two methods of limiting the foreign tax credit concluded in a 1976 report that the overall limitation method was preferable to the per-country method, primarily because of its lesser complexity.

9. CED previously called for favorable consideration of the treatment currently in effect, under which only research and development expenses directly related and traceable to foreign earnings are treated as a deduction from foreign source income. See our policy statement <u>Stimulating Technological Progress</u>, January 1980, p. 41.

Adverse Effects on International Competitiveness

With increasing international interdependence, the ability of U.S. industry to compete effectively in international markets is critically important to the economy. The Administration's tax reform plan includes a number of proposals that are likely to enhance U.S. international competitiveness, including particularly the provisions for lowering the corporate tax rate and the dividend-paid deduction. However, we are concerned that various other features of the reform proposal are likely to have adverse effects on the international competitiveness of U.S. industry.

First, as indicated in the previous section, the Administration's proposals for a revised capital cost recovery system, the repeal of the investment tax credit, the recapture provision, and other changes related to the treatment of capital investment are on balance likely to worsen U.S. international competitiveness, at least in the short run.

Second, to the extent that the reform plan implies a risk of prospective revenue shortfalls that would add to the budget deficit, upward pressures on interest rates and dollar exchange rates would be increased, with corresponding adverse effects on U.S. international competitiveness.

Third, we are concerned about a number of specific proposals relating to international taxation. We are particularly concerned about the Administration's proposal to change the method of computing the foreign tax credit from the current "overall" method to a country-by-country limitation.

This proposed change would place U.S. firms at a competitive disadvantage relative to foreign multinational corporations whose home countries either exempt foreign source income from tax or allow the

In our view, this special emphasis on equipment is justified for a number of reasons. Together with research and development, new equipment purchases are often the vehicle for introducing new technology into production processes. Very frequently, the benefits of such new technology are greater to society as a whole than to the producers who introduce it. Moreover, for many firms -- particularly in the manufacturing sector -- the speedy introduction of new technology is critically important if they are to remain internationally competitive.

One approach toward achieving the above objectives that could be considered would involve an adjustment in the depreciation "basis" for equipment that would be designed to approach the equivalent of expensing such capital investment outlays by raising the discounted present value of the recovery allowances up to the original purchase price of the investment.

A second possible approach would be to make a depreciation basis adjustment that is more favorable to investment in equipment than the President's proposal but that does not go so far as to be fully equivalent to expensing when calculated on the standard assumption that the item is equity financed. This approach would reduce the chances that negative tax rates might result.

A third approach, which would produce a result that is approximately equivalent to that achieved by the first of the two options cited above, would entail preserving some form of the investment tax credit at about half of its present rates, along with the proposed CCRS schedule. The Treasury's concerns about the relation between the ITC and possible tax sheltering activities could be met by some stretching out of the ITC benefits over several years instead of having such benefits accrue all at the front end of an investment as is currently the case.

value of tax payments than is justified by the Administration's expressed rationale.[7] Moreover, this totally unprecedented provision would heighten uncertainties concerning the value of future depreciation and, in turn, inhibit decisions to invest. <u>Given these serious disadvantages, we believe the wisest course is to eliminate completely the recapture provision in the reform proposal.</u>

Over and above the generally adverse cash flow effect of the proposed reform, its termination of the investment tax credit and switch in the treatment of depreciation from the Accelerated Cost Recovery System (ACRS) to the Capital Cost Recovery System (CCRS) increases the effective cost of investment in equipment to the user.*

The President has already acknowledged some concern in this area. The original reform proposal released by the Treasury last fall implied sizable adverse effects on investment in equipment. Subsequent revisions in the depreciation schedules incorporated into the President's proposal helped to ease these adverse effects. <u>But we believe still further modifications are needed to achieve the objective of no significant net adverse effect on equipment apart from reducing instances of negative effective tax rates.</u>

---

7. See "Recapture of Excess Depreciation: What are the Issues?" by C. Clinton Stretch and Emil M. Sunley of Deloitte, Haskins & Sells in Tax Notes, June 24, 1985, pp. 1501-1505. Stretch and Sunley estimate that for five-year property, the proposed recapture provision would collect 25 percent more revenue than could be justified by the Administration's rationale. For fifteen-year property, the revenue collected would be triple the amount that could be justified on such a basis.

*See memorandum by W. BRUCE THOMAS (page 27).

machines that introduce new technology into the productive process in our factories, offices and distribution systems. Business investment in plant and equipment has risen very substantially from its low point in the 1981-82 recession, but it must rise still further to generate the greater economic growth and enhanced competitive capability that our country needs.[6]

In contrast, we believe the combined effect of eliminating the investment tax credit, of the new depreciation rules, and of the ACRS windfall recapture provision would negatively affect some of the most productive areas of new capital investment, especially in equipment.*

The heavy onus on investment in the next few years results chiefly from the sharp reduction in corporate cash flow. A major factor in this connection is the ACRS windfall recapture provision, which is estimated to generate a total of about $60 billion in additional revenue for the Treasury from 1986 to 1989. This provision is explained as an effort to "recapture" the "windfall profit" generated by the beneficial effect of a lower marginal tax rate on deferred corporate tax liabilities. It is bad tax principle to establish provisions that have the effect of enacting retroactive tax laws. Furthermore, in this case the proposed discounting formula appears so harsh as to recapture far more in present

---

6. The CED policy statement, <u>Strategy for U.S. Industrial Competitiveness</u>, has addressed a series of policy issues that are crucial in rebuilding U.S. international competitiveness.

*See memoranda by FRANK P. DOYLE (page 20), THOMAS J. EYERMAN (page 21), and CHARLES W. PARRY (page 24).

recovery provisions will result in significant and successively rising revenue losses after 1990.[4] Other published studies (such as one by Data Resources, Inc., which is based on the analysis of both corporate and individual tax provisions) estimate even larger long-term revenue shortfalls.[5]

There are also some questions whether even the revised Administration plan would be fully revenue-neutral over the next five years. Unlike the Treasury's 1984 plan, the President's proposal makes no provision for transition rules in connection with the proposed elimination of the Investment Tax Credit, although the need for such transition rules is specifically acknowledged. Some form of "binding contract" rule to deal with this problem could cut tax revenues by a cumulative total of about $8 billion below the Reagan proposal estimates during the initial years after adoption of the proposal. Additional questions arise because some provisions that are counted on to raise substantial revenue have encountered strong criticism and may be difficult to implement.

Concerns about Treatment of Investment

We lay great stress on the effects of the proposed changes on investment because of the key role investment plays in our economy. It increases the productive power of American workers.* It provides the

---

4. Staff study on Tax Reform Proposals: Taxation of Capital Income, Joint Committee on Taxation, Washington, D.C., August 8, 1985, pp. 85-96.

5. Data Resources, Inc., Tax Reform II: The President's Tax Proposals for Fairness, Growth, and Simplicity, testimony by Dr. Roger E. Brinner, June 11, 1985.

*See memorandum by JAMES Q. RIORDAN (page 25).

At the same time, as we also have said, several features of the proposal fall significantly short of CED's objectives. Of greatest concern are its effects on revenues, on investment, and on competitiveness.

Revenue Concerns

The Administration's tax reform proposal presented in May 1985 would have resulted in a cumulative revenue loss of $25 billion from 1986 to 1990, according to estimates by the Congressional Joint Committee on Taxation. Various revisions in the plan announced by Secretary of the Treasury Baker at the end of August are designed to produce approximate revenue neutrality of the proposal over the first five years of its operation.

While we have reservations about the specific changes proposed to achieve this revenue result, we welcome the Administration's expressed commitment to producing a revenue-neutral plan. We are, however, concerned that even with the recent revisions, the Administration plan could, in fact, result in significant revenue losses, at least over the longer term.

Thus, a recent Congressional Budget Office staff study estimates that the general corporate tax provisions in the President's proposal would add at least $16 billion to the annual budget deficit by 1995, with the gap widening toward $20 billion a year by 2000.[3] A subsequent study by the Congressional Joint Committee on Taxation (which does not include specific revenue estimates) similarly suggests that the proposed capital

---

3. Congressional Budget Office, Analysis of Long-Term Revenue Impacts of the President's Tax Reform Plan, staff working paper, June 1985.

among objectives and among design principles where these are in some conflict.* Given this constraint, however, it remains desirable to choose a reform plan that adheres to the foregoing objectives and principles to the maximum extent feasible.**

PRESIDENT REAGAN'S TAX REFORM PROPOSAL

As we have indicated, the President's proposal in several respects represents a substantial improvement over the current system and accords more nearly with our stated principles than current law.*** More specifically:

- It lowers marginal rates substantially for both individuals and business. We believe this is highly desirable and ought to be preserved as much as is possible in keeping with the other objectives of the tax reform and the need to bring about further substantial reductions in the budget deficit.

- It establishes the principle of not taxing dividends twice. This is, however, limited to only 10 percent of the dividends paid.

- It introduces an index factor for inflation into future depreciation schedules, thus beginning to reduce the distorting effects of inflation on investment decisions.

- It reduces some of the disparities in effective tax rates paid on the same types of income.

- It simplifies the income tax system for many individuals and would ease somewhat the administration of the system. It is, however, more complicated for most businesses and for many of those who itemize deductions.

- It eliminates a number of nonproductive tax preferences.

---

*See memorandum by ELMER B. STAATS (page 27).
** See memorandum by LYLE EVERINGHAM (page 21).
*** See memoranda by RALPH E. BAILEY (page 19) and JAMES Q. RIORDAN (page 24).

term. In addition, there should be a transition plan that minimizes disruption and is practically achievable. The transition plan should provide clear direction to allow individuals and institutions to plan their economic activity both during and after the transition.

- <u>Treatment of Income</u>. Income, however defined, of similar nature should receive similar tax treatment. Moving the tax system in this direction would serve the objectives of both equity and economic efficiency.

- <u>Economic Efficiency</u>. In the interest of minimizing deterrents to economic efficiency and growth, the system should interfere as little as possible with the economic choices made by individuals or institutions. These choices would, of course, include the ones between consumption and saving, operating and capital outlays, greater or lesser work effort, and among types of investment.

- <u>United States in the World Economy</u>. The U.S. tax system should not be detrimental to the U.S. role in the world economy.

- <u>Inflation</u>. The system should as far as possible remove the effects of inflation on the tax burden borne by taxpayers.

- <u>Direct Charges for Services</u>. When special services are provided to particular classes of taxpayers, these costs should, to the extent possible, be charged to those users.

We recognize that no tax reform plan can be expected to conform fully with all of these design principles. Some deviations from individual principles can be expected in practice, both because of pragmatic considerations and because of conflicting implications of particular principles. Any final decisions regarding the type of tax reform to be adopted must involve judgments about desirable tradeoffs

Finally, and perhaps most importantly, tax reform needs to proceed under a strategic discipline that can help keep tax changes oriented to these four fundamental objectives. There will always be pressures from special interests to put self-serving changes in the system. We believe the following principles, rigorously used to test proposed changes, can help policy makers resist pressures to deviate from the basic objectives and maximize the likelihood that only the most worthy provisions are put in place.

- Primary Purpose. The tax system should be used primarily to raise revenue.* The main reason for the present complexity of the code is that it has been overburdened with provisions to achieve many other objectives.** Without the discipline of this principle, simplicity is impossible.

- Low Rates. With due regard to ability to pay, the system should include as many taxpayers and as few exceptions as possible, thus allowing the lowest tax rates to raise a given needed level of revenue. Low rates minimize the economic distortions inherent in any tax system.

- Accountability. The amount, and to the extent possible, the effect of all taxes imposed should be clearly visible. This will serve as a check on the natural tendency of politicians to increase revenues without adequate prior interaction with taxpaying entities.***

- Stability over the Long Run and During Transition. The system should be the best we can design to achieve the objectives on a long-term basis, and should be kept as stable as possible over the long

---

*See memorandum by ROBERT R. NATHAN (page 23).
**See memorandum by ELMER B. STAATS (page 27).
***See memorandum by PHILIP M. KLUTZNICK (page 22).

System (ACRS), and of the new depreciation schedule could, we believe, adversely affect our nation's economic growth and the competitive capability of a significant share of our industry. We believe that for the economy to benefit ultimately from tax reform embodying lower marginal tax rates, these disruptive effects on productive investment will have to be minimized.* The following pages present our recommendations for this purpose as well as balancing provisions to assure overall revenue neutrality.**

Desirable Objectives and Principles of Tax Reform

We believe any tax reform ought to strive to meet four fundamental objectives:

- generate revenues effectively;

- be as simple and clear as possible for purposes of taxpayer understanding, ease of compliance and efficiency of administration;

- be equitable and perceived as such -- particularly, taxpayers in comparable circumstances should be treated the same way; and***

- not adversely affect economic efficiency, sound economic growth, cyclical stability, and U.S. international competitiveness.

We believe that the development of any new tax system must be comprehensive and must involve an open discussion of the issues and of the actual and potential impact of the proposed changes. Basic reform also needs to have clearly delineated transition provisions in order to minimize the disruptive effects that any reform is likely to create.

---

*See memorandum by CHARLES W. PARRY (page 23).
**See memorandum by ROGER B. SMITH (page 26).
***See memorandum by ROBERT R. NATHAN (page 23).

Our nation needs to be wary of unduly burdening productive investment, for it is a prime factor enhancing the competitive capability of U.S. industry and generating vigorous national economic growth.*

The damage to capital investment inflicted by higher budget deficits and more burdensome tax provisions would be felt with particular force in the industrial sector of the economy, which has been especially hard hit by the emergence of the huge U.S. foreign trade deficit and widespread job losses. Conversely, actions to contain and reduce the budget deficit and to reform the tax system in ways that are conducive to needed increases in productive investment and innovation should strengthen the industrial sector and preserve and expand job opportunities.[2]

In light of this background, it is our judgment that tax reform should be carefully designed so as to have <u>no more</u> detrimental effect on productive investment than the present system.** This does not mean that the system should not be revised to eliminate negative effective tax rates wherever possible.

Given this conviction, we are concerned over several specific provisions in the Administration's proposal that, taken together, can have a potentially detrimental effect on capital investment. The combined effects of eliminating the investment tax credit, of the windfall recapture provision applicable to the Accelerated Cost Recovery

---

2. For a detailed discussion of these interrelated effects, see our 1984 policy statements <u>Fighting Federal Deficits: The Time for Hard Choices</u>, pp. 12-17 and <u>Strategy for U.S. Industrial Competitiveness</u>, chapters 1 and 3.

*See memorandum by ROBERT R. NATHAN (page 22).
** See memoranda by JACK F. BENNETT (page 19) and JAMES Q. RIORDAN (page 24).

Budget Resolution will go part of the way toward achieving this objective. However, full action on CED's or a similar approach remains urgent if we are to succeed in maintaining a vital and growing economy.

This policy statement focuses on the desirable objectives and principles of tax reform and, in the light of these principles, assesses those features of President Reagan's tax reform proposal that are of special relevance to productive capital investment, innovation, and sound economic growth.[1]

In several respects, the President's tax reform proposal represents a substantial improvement over the current system in terms of these perspectives. However, we have a number of concerns about the plan.* We believe two aspects of the proposal require priority attention.

First, although the revisions in the Administration's proposal announced in early September 1985 would technically make the proposal revenue neutral in its first five years of operation, we are concerned that certain features of the proposal could nevertheless result in a net loss of revenues and increase the already large federal deficit -- to some extent in the early years and more significantly over the long run.

Second, we believe that in addition to this deficit effect, a number of the proposed changes cited will adversely affect investment relative to consumption and will hamper U.S. industrial competitiveness.**

---

1. Our comments in this report relate to the Administration's tax reform proposal issued in May 1985, as revised in a letter by Secretary of the Treasury Baker to House Ways and Means Committee Chairman Rostenkowski dated August 31, 1985.

*See memorandum by WILLIAM S. WOODSIDE (page 28).
**See memorandum by LYLE EVERINGHAM (page 20).

TAX REFORM FOR A PRODUCTIVE ECONOMY

Introduction

We believe that there is a clear need for basic tax reform to make the U.S. tax structure significantly simpler and fairer, as well as more conducive to economic efficiency, sound economic growth, and U.S. international competitiveness. Our current federal income tax system is widely perceived to be unfair, too complicated, and conducive to too many nonproductive investments. It is also perceived to discourage work and to distort economic decisions, with respect both to domestic and to international transactions. We believe reform is essential to ensure the continued integrity of our voluntary system of tax compliance, to end the growing incidence of tax evasion, and to distribute the burden of taxation more equitably among those able to pay.

We strongly believe, however, that tax reform should not be allowed to work against actions critically needed to reduce prospective U.S. budget deficits.* CED has repeatedly stated its conviction that these deficits constitute the single greatest threat to the economic health of this country that we now face. The 1984 CED policy statement, Fighting Federal Deficits: The Time for Hard Choices, set forth a comprehensive plan to bring the budget to near balance by the end of the decade. If vigorously implemented, the recently passed Congressional

---

*See memoranda by WILLIAM F. MAY (page 22), ROBERT R. NATHAN (page 22), and ELMER B. STAATS (page 27).

We are also deeply grateful to the Alfred P. Sloan Foundation and the John M. Olin Foundation for their generous support of the basic assessments of a sound U.S. tax structure which helped support this project.

We trust that the policy statement we have brought forth can help advance a broader public consensus covering the most productive design for tax reform.

William F. May
Chairman
Research and Policy Committee

Economic Research, whom CED commissioned to develop a careful analysis of the effects on the economy of various reform options. His work, which benefited from discussions with a task force also chaired by Dean Phypers, will be published in 1986 by Harvard University Press under the title <u>Untangling the Income Tax</u>.

The CED Subcommittee on Tax Policy first concentrated on what should be the basic objectives and principles of tax reform. In the light of these principles, it then assessed certain specific areas of tax policy where CED as an organization could help promote consensus through a combination of careful analysis and an examination of the lessons of corporate experience. The results, completed in September before the current round of Congressional proposals, are set forth in the following pages. The fact that the Subcommittee has succeeded in achieving such a degree of consensus on so divisive a subject is a tribute to Dean Phypers and the members of his committee.

Acknowledgments

I would like to thank the extraordinarily able group of members and advisors who served on the subcommittee that prepared this report. A list of their names appears on page iv.

The work of this subcommittee was greatly aided by the analysis of the Administration's first and second set of tax recommendations that was prepared by a CED task force of experts chaired by Frederick Deming, senior vice president and economist for Chemical Bank. A list of the individuals serving on this task force appears on page v.

We are also grateful for the sophisticated understanding of tax issues and literary craftmanship brought to this study by project director Frank W. Schiff, vice president and chief economist of CED.

PURPOSE OF THIS STATEMENT

Few issues are so widely endorsed at a general level and so bitterly disputed on specifics as tax reform. Taxes and tax reform are among the most complex and controversial issues facing policy makers and the public.

One reason it is so difficult to reach agreement on the specifics of tax reform is that taxes affect individuals and institutions in so many different ways. One person's tax reform is often another's burden, and efforts to remove an inequity for one taxpayer or industry may impose hardship on another.

In addition, the U.S. tax system is less a system than an intricate and sometimes contradictory collection of policies and rules that have complex, wide ranging effects on the workings of the American economy. As a result of comprehending the net effect of even one tax change can be a challenging task.

The Committee for Economic Development has a long standing interest in taxes and their impact on the U.S. economy. Several years ago, it became clear to CED's trustees that even with growing public support for major reform, there was a significant need for a clearer understanding of basic tax issues and a companion need to reduce differences of views based on this enhanced understanding.

Under the guidance of Dean P. Phypers, senior vice president of IBM Corporation, the CED Subcommittee on Tax Policy analyzed the extraordinary diversity of issues and potential problems that tax reform poses. This effort was greatly assisted by the analytical insights brought by Professor David Bradford of Princeton University and the National Bureau of

PROJECT DIRECTOR

FRANK W. SCHIFF
Vice Chairman and Chief Economist
Committee for Economic Development

PROJECT STAFF

SEONG H. PARK
Economist
Committee for Economic Development

BETTY S. TRIMBLE
Assistant Office Manager
Committee for Economic Development

BARBARA P. WILLARD
Administrative Assistant
Committee for Economic Development

PEGGY MORRISSETTE
Deputy Secretary, Research and Policy
  Committee
Committee for Economic Development

TASK FORCE ON EVALUATIONS OF ECONOMIC EFFECTS OF TREASURY TAX REFORM PROPOSALS

Chairman
FREDERICK W. DEMING
Senior Vice President and
  Economist
Chemical Bank

ROBERT L. ASHBY
Director of Taxes
Northern Telecom, Inc.

NORMAN BENSLEY
Vice President and Assistant
  General Counsel
New York Life Insurance Co.

WILLIAM T. BOEHM
Director of Economic Research and
  Commodity Analysis
The Kroger Co.

CLAUDE BRINEGAR
Senior Vice President and Director
Unocal Corporation

WILLIAM G. DAKIN
Tax Counsel
Mobil Corporation

DAVID R. DILLEY
Chief Economist
U.S. Steel Corporation

THOMAS DuBOS
Tax Legislative Counsel
Mobil Corporation

RONALD O. DURANT
Economics Consultant
Corporate Planning Department
Exxon Company USA

JAMES HANSON
Chief Economist
Corporate Planning Department
Exxon Corporation

MICHAEL HENRY
Director, Business and Tax Public Policy
Sun Company, Inc.

JAMES HODGE
Economist
IBM Corporation

DENNIS HOOVER
District Manager
Economic Analysis
AT&T

CHARLES R. HULTEN
Professor and Chairman
Department of Economics
University of Maryland

ALAN KELLNER
Business Economist
General Foods Corporation

BRIAN KIDNEY
Director, Federal Relations
Pacific Telesis Group

ROBERT MATTSON
Director of Taxes
IBM Corporation

KARL M. MAYER
Chief Economist
ITT Corporation

JOHN E. McCOY
Manager, Tax Accounting Operations
General Electric Corporation

DAVID C. MUNRO
General Director, Macro and International
  Economics
General Motors Corporation

MARTIN SOOPER
Director, Tax
Pacific Telesis Group

EMIL M. SUNLEY
Director of Tax Analysis
Deloitte, Haskins & Sells

THOMAS E. SWANSTROM
Chief Economist
Sears, Roebuck and Co.

SUBCOMMITTEE ON TAX POLICY

Chairman
DEAN P. PHYPERS
Senior Vice President
IBM Corporation

ROY L. ASH
Los Angeles, California

*JACK F. BENNETT
Senior Vice President
Exxon Corporation

THEODORE A. BURTIS
Chairman of the Board
Sun Company, Inc.

JOHN B. CAVE
Executive Vice President—Finance
McGraw-Hill, Inc.

ROBERT A. CHARPIE
President
Cabot Corporation

*FRANK P. DOYLE
Senior Vice President
General Electric Company

*LYLE EVERINGHAM
Chairman of the Board and Chief
  Executive Officer
The Kroger Co.

HARRY L. FREEMAN
Executive Vice President, Corporate
  Affairs and Communications
American Express Company

W. GRANT GREGORY
Chairman of the Board
Touche Ross & Co.

DONALD E. GUINN
Chairman and Chief Executive Officer
Pacific Telesis Group

FRED L. HARTLEY
Chairman and President
Unocal Corporation

FRANKLIN A. LINDSAY
Chairman
Vectron, Inc.

*ROBERT R. NATHAN
Chairman
Robert R. Nathan Associates, Inc.

NORMA PACE
Senior Vice President
American Paper Institute

PETER G. PETERSON
Chairman
Peterson, Jacobs & Company

DONALD C. PLATTEN
Chairman, Executive Committee
Chemical Bank

*JAMES Q. RIORDAN
Senior Vice President
Mobil Corporation

DONALD K. ROSS
Chairman of the Board
New York Life Insurance Company

DONALD B. SMILEY
Chairman, Finance Committee
R. H. Macy & Co., Inc.

PHILIP L. SMITH
President and Chief
  Operating Officer
General Foods Corporation

*ELMER B. STAATS
Former Comptroller General of the
  United States
Washington, D.C.

MORRIS TANENBAUM
Executive Vice President
AT&T

*W. BRUCE THOMAS
Vice Chairman of Administration and
  Chief Financial Officer
United States Steel Corporation

[1]M. CABELL WOODWARD, JR.
Vice Chairman and Chief Financial
  Officer
ITT Corporation

Nontrustee Member[2]

RICHARD M. JONES
Vice Chairman of the Board and
  Chief Financial Officer
Sears, Roebuck & Co.

*Voted to approve the policy statement but submitted memoranda of comment, reservation, or dissent.
[1]Did not participate in the voting due to illness.
[2]Nontrustee members take part in all discussions of the statement but do not vote on it.

ADVISORS

DAVID F. BRADFORD
Professor
Woodrow Wilson School
Princeton University

FREDERICK W. DEMING
Senior Vice President and
  Economist
Chemical Bank

HARVEY GALPER
Senior Fellow
The Brookings Institution

RICHARD GOODE
Washington, D.C.

JAMES HANSON
Chief Economist
Exxon Corporation

CHARLES R. HULTEN
Professor and Chairman of
  Economics
University of Maryland

KENNETH McLENNAN
Vice President and Director of
  Industrial Studies
Committee for Economic Development

NATHANIEL M. SEMPLE
Vice President and Secretary, Research
  and Policy Committee
Committee for Economic Development

EMIL M. SUNLEY
Director of Tax Analysis
Deloitte, Haskins & Sells

RESEARCH AND POLICY COMMITTEE

Chairman
WILLIAM F. MAY

Vice Chairmen
WILLIAM S. EDGERLY/*Education and Social and Urban Development*
RODERICK M. HILLS/*Government*
JAMES W. McKEE, JR./*International Economic Studies*
ROCCO C. SICILIANO/*National Economy*

ROY L. ASH
Los Angeles, California

*RALPH E. BAILEY, Chairman and Chief Executive Officer
Conoco Inc.

WARREN L. BATTS, President
Dart & Kraft, Inc.

*JACK F. BENNETT, Senior Vice President
Exxon Corporation

THEODORE A. BURTIS, Chairman of the Board
Sun Company, Inc.

OWEN B. BUTLER, Chairman of the Board
The Procter & Gamble Company

FLETCHER L. BYROM, Retired Chairman
Koppers Company, Inc.

ROBERT J. CARLSON, Chairman, President and Chief Executive Officer
BMC Inc.

RAFAEL CARRION, JR., Chairman of the Board
Banco Popular de Puerto Rico

JOHN B. CAVE, Executive Vice President–Finance
McGraw-Hill, Inc.

ROBERT A. CHARPIE, President
Cabot Corporation

[1]ROBERT CIZIK, Chairman and President
Cooper Industries, Inc.

EMILIO G. COLLADO, Executive Chairman
International Planning Corporation

D. RONALD DANIEL, Managing Director
McKinsey & Company, Inc.

RONALD R. DAVENPORT, Chairman of the Board
Sheridan Broadcasting Corporation

PETER A. DEROW, President
CBS/Publishing Group

*FRANK P. DOYLE, Senior Vice President
General Electric Company

W. D. EBERLE, President
Manchester Associates, Ltd.

WILLIAM S. EDGERLY, Chairman of the Board and President
State Street Bank and Trust Company

[2]THOMAS J. EYERMAN, Partner
Skidmore, Owings & Merrill

JOHN H. FILER, Partner
Tyler, Cooper & Alcorn

EDMUND B. FITZGERALD, Chairman and Chief Executive Officer
Northern Telecom Limited

ROBERT E. FRAZER, Chairman
The Dayton Power and Light Company

DONALD E. GUINN, Chairman and Chief Executive Officer
Pacific Telesis Group

RICHARD W. HANSELMAN, Chairman, President and Chief Executive Officer
Genesco Inc.

PHILIP M. HAWLEY, Chairman of the Board
Carter Hawley Hale Stores, Inc.

RODERICK M. HILLS, Of Counsel
Latham, Watkins & Hills

ROBERT C. HOLLAND, President
Committee for Economic Development

LEON C. HOLT, JR., Vice Chairman and Chief Administrative Officer
Air Products and Chemicals, Inc.

[3]JAMES L. KETELSEN, Chairman and Chief Executive Officer
Tenneco Inc.

CHARLES M. KITTRELL, Executive Vice President
Phillips Petroleum Company

*PHILIP M. KLUTZNICK, Senior Partner
Klutznick Investments

RALPH LAZARUS, Chairman Emeritus
Federated Department Stores, Inc.

FRANKLIN A. LINDSAY, Chairman
Vectron, Inc.

HOWARD M. LOVE, Chairman and Chief Executive Officer
National Intergroup, Inc.

ROBERT W. LUNDEEN, Chairman of the Board
The Dow Chemical Company

*WILLIAM F. MAY, President
Statue of Liberty — Ellis Island Foundation, Inc.

ALONZO L. McDONALD, Chairman and Chief Executive Officer
Avenir Group, Inc.

JAMES W. McKEE, JR., Chairman
CPC International Inc.

ROBERT E. MERCER, Chairman of the Board
The Goodyear Tire & Rubber Company

RUBEN F. METTLER, Chairman of the Board and Chief Executive Officer
TRW Inc.

STEVEN MULLER, President
The Johns Hopkins University

NORMA PACE, Senior Vice President
American Paper Institute

VICTOR H. PALMIERI, Chairman
The Palmieri Company

*CHARLES W. PARRY, Chairman and Chief Executive Officer
Aluminum Company of America

DEAN P. PHYPERS, Senior Vice President
IBM Corporation

LELAND S. PRUSSIA, Chairman of the Board
Bank of America N.T. & S.A.

*JAMES Q. RIORDAN, Senior Vice President
Mobil Corporation

FRANCIS C. ROONEY, JR., Chairman of the Board
Melville Corporation

HENRY B. SCHACHT, Chairman of the Board and Chief Executive Officer
Cummins Engine Company, Inc.

DONNA E. SHALALA, President
Hunter College

PHILIP L. SMITH, President and Chief Operating Officer
General Foods Corporation

RICHARD M. SMITH, Vice Chairman
Bethlehem Steel Corporation

*ROGER B. SMITH, Chairman
General Motors Corporation

*ELMER B. STAATS, Former Comptroller General of the United States
Washington, D.C.

WILLIAM C. STOLK
Bridgeport, Connecticut

ANTHONY P. TERRACCIANO, Executive Vice President—Global Banking
The Chase Manhattan Bank, N.A.

WALTER N. THAYER, Chairman
Whitney Communications Company

*W. BRUCE THOMAS, Vice Chairman of Administration and Chief Financial Officer
United States Steel Corporation

SIDNEY J. WEINBERG, JR., Partner
Goldman, Sachs & Co.

[4]ALTON W. WHITEHOUSE, JR., Chairman
The Standard Oil Company (Ohio)

RICHARD D. WOOD, Chairman of the Board
Eli Lilly and Company

*WILLIAM S. WOODSIDE, Chairman
American Can Company

---

*Voted to approve the policy statement but submitted memoranda of comment, reservation, or dissent. Memoranda begin on page 19.
[1]Did not participate in the voting due to travel outside this country.
[2]Voted to disapprove this statement and submitted memoranda of comment, reservation, or dissent.
[3]Voted to disapprove this statement.
[4]Abstained.

RESPONSIBILITY FOR CED STATEMENTS ON NATIONAL POLICY

The Committee for Economic Development is an independent research and educational organization of 225 business executives and educators. CED is nonprofit, nonpartisan, and nonpolitical. Its purpose is to propose policies that will help to bring about steady economic growth at high employment and reasonably stable prices, increase productivity and living standards, provide greater and more equal opportunity for every citizen, and improve the quality of life for all. A more complete description of CED appears on page 29.

All CED policy recommendations must have the approval of trustees on the Research and Policy Committee. This committee is directed under the bylaws to "initiate studies into the principles of business policy and of public policy which will foster the full contribution by industry and commerce to the attainment and maintenance" of the objectives stated above. The bylaws emphasize that "all research is to be thoroughly objective in character, and the approach in each instance is to be from the standpoint of the general welfare and not from that of any special political or economic group." The committee is aided by a Research Advisory Board of leading social scientists and by a small permanent professional staff.

The Research and Policy Committee does not attempt to pass judgment on any pending specific legislative proposals; its purpose is to urge careful consideration of the objectives set forth in this statement and of the best means of accomplishing those objectives.

Each statement is preceded by extensive discussions, meetings, and exchange of memoranda. The research is undertaken by a subcommittee, assisted by advisors chosen for their competence in the field under study. The members and advisors of the subcommittee that prepared this statement are listed on page iv.

The full Research and Policy Committee participates in the drafting of recommendations. Likewise, the trustees on the drafting subcommittee vote to approve or disapprove a policy statement, and they share with the Research and Policy Committee the privilege of submitting individual comments for publication, as noted on pages 19 through 28 of this statement.

Except for the members of the Research and Policy Committee and the responsible subcommittee, the recommendations presented herein are not necessarily endorsed by other trustees or by the advisors, contributors, staff members, or others associated with CED.

CONTENTS

Responsibility for CED Statements on National Policy	ii
Purpose of this Statement	vi
TAX REFORM FOR A PRODUCTIVE ECONOMY	1
Introduction	1
Desirable Objectives and Principles of Tax Reform	4
PRESIDENT REAGAN'S TAX REFORM PROPOSAL	7
Revenue Concerns	8
Concerns about Treatment of Investment	9
Adverse Effects on International Competitiveness	13
Making Up Revenue Shortfalls	15
Memoranda of Comment, Reservation, or Dissent	19
Objectives of the Committee for Economic Development	29